What Do You Think?

Is Genetic Research A Threat?

John Meany

Heinemann Library
Chicago, Illinois

© 2009 Heinemann Library
a division of Pearson Inc.
Chicago, Illinois

Customer Service 888-454-2279
Visit our website at www.heinemannraintree.com

Editorial: Andrew Farrow and Rebecca Vickers
Design: Philippa Jenkins
Picture Research: Melissa Allison, Ruth Blair, and Virginia Stroud-Lewis
Production: Alison Parsons

Originated by Heinemann Library
Printed and bound in China

13 12 11 10 09
10 9 8 7 6 5 4 3 2 1

Library of Congress Cataloging-in-Publication Data
Meany, John.
  Is genetic research a threat? / John Meany.
     p. cm. -- (What do you think?)
  Includes bibliographical references and index.
  ISBN 978-1-4329-1674-9 (hc)
  1. Genetics--Social aspects. 2. Genetic engineering--Social aspects. I. Title.
  QH438.7.M43 2008
  174'.957--dc22
                                        2008014750

Acknowledgments
The author and publishers are grateful to the following for permission to reproduce copyright material: © Alamy pp. /Sally and Richard Greenhill **36, 40**, /imagestopshop/Lisa Valder **26**, /PhotoStockFile/Paul Wayne Wilson **48**, /Frances Roberts **42**; © Corbis pp. /Bill Barksdale **44**, /Andrew Brookes **13**, /Dave Ellis/Pool/CNP **32**, /Randy Faris **29**, /Firefly Productions **18**, /Reuters **21**, /Reuters/Jacques Brinon/Pool **6**, /Reuters/Juda Ngwenya **31**, /H. Schmid/zefa **9**, /Pawel Wysocki/ Hemis **25**, /Sygma **15**; © with kind permission of Prof. Paul Erhlich/Stanford University p. **47**; © Getty Images pp. /Photodisc **10**, /Time & Life Pictures **23**; © The Kobal Collection/Polygram/Spelling p. **35**; © Science Photo Library pp. /AJ Photo **41**, /IP, Laurent/Lesache **37**, /J.C Tessier/Publiphoto Diffussion **38**, /Trick Dumas/Eurelios **4**; © Kate Shuster p. **51**.

Cover photograph of an artist's conceptual image of human clones reproduced with permission of © Corbis/zefa/Matthias Kulka and © istockphoto.com/Mark Stay.

The publishers would like to thank Dr. Michael Reiss for his assistance in the preparation of this book.

Every effort has been made to contact copyright holders of any material reproduced in this book. Any omissions will be rectified in subsequent printings if notice is given to the publisher.

Table Of Contents

Some words are printed in bold, **like this**. You can find out what they mean in the Glossary on pages 54–55.

> *The power of technology*

Governments and private companies spend many billions of dollars in health research each year. Scientists have made important discoveries in genetics and **biotechnology**. The power of this research is growing quickly—there are new possibilities for human and nonhuman life, as well as new risks.

Understanding Genetic Research And Engineering

In 2003, researchers completed one of the most important scientific projects in history—a **genome** map of a human being. This was called the Human Genome Project. The goal of this research was to identify all human **genes**, about 25,000 of them. The Human Genome Project explored the basic building blocks of life, including **DNA**, chromosomes, proteins, and genes. The project took 13 years, and it became the model for other genome investigations of plants and animals. The purpose of the Human Genome Project was to understand how the **cells** that make up a human being create a living organism. With this knowledge, it would be easier for biologists, physicians, and other scientists to study human health. This was important information. Missing or broken genes in individuals are responsible for thousands of diseases. Research might be able to save millions of lives. But knowledge of the basics of human life also had risks. Would scientists be able to manufacture life? Could they produce stronger "designer" athletes, brilliant "baby Einsteins," or copies of humans? Could genetic knowledge help make biological weapons that could be used against specific ethnic or racial groups?

Genetic research has the potential for significant benefits, but it might also be a threat. Should more genetic research be permitted and what kinds should be allowed? What do you think?

Critical thinking and debating skills

When trying to understand all the aspects of a difficult and complex subject, such as genetic research, the skills involved in critical thinking are very important. These are careful listening, note taking, public speaking, argumentation, and **refutation**. All these can help to identify important ideas, form opinions, and reply to others. Developing and using these skills will allow you to better explain and defend your opinions on the value of genetic research.

Argumentation

Let's see how an **argument** works, using the following two claims about people:
1. They have opinions.
2. They generally prefer their own opinions to the opinions of others.

Most of the public would agree with these claims. But if people simply prefer their own opinions on a topic, how can others ever change their opinions? How can anyone persuade them? What can motivate them to change their views?

It is challenging to try to persuade others about a new idea. It is certainly not enough to have a "good idea." That is because others will also have their own opinions on the same topic; they will have their own "good ideas." Why should they listen to new ones? That is the reason why, to be persuasive, a person has to have a better idea. This can be expressed as an argument.

An argument is more than a simple opinion—it is the best possible expression of an opinion. It is both well reasoned and supported by evidence. Ultimately, effective arguments are developed and used to prove that an opinion is both more likely to be true than false and more credible than conflicting opinions from others. Better ideas can be persuasive.

What is an argument?

An argument is an idea that includes an assertion, reasoning, and evidence. It is easy to identify an argument by the letters **A—R—E**, which represent these three parts. If it has **A—R—E**, it is an argument.

An assertion is an opinion. It is a simple statement that a person is ready to prove. Examples of assertions include:
◆ I am tired.
◆ I like to travel.
◆ Diseases have serious economic costs.

Reasoning is the logical examination of an opinion. It is the speaker's explanation of the assertion. It answers the question—WHY? Why are you tired?

Why do you like to travel? Why do diseases hurt the economy? Here are the same assertions, with the addition of reasoning:

- I am tired. There was so much noise from the neighbors last night that I only got three hours of sleep and I need at least eight hours to be fully rested.
- I like to travel. I enjoy meeting different people and visiting places that I could only imagine. The experiences from travel make me realize how much I have to learn about the world, which helps motivate me to study.
- Diseases have serious economic costs. Diseases reduce the number of days that people are able to go to work. Sick people do not go to work. Because diseases reduce work, there are not as many products made or customers served. Diseases have a significant effect on the economy.

> *Using critical thinking skills*

Argumentation, debate, and refutation are used to challenge opinions, produce better ideas, and make new laws. Serious debate helps improve the lives of citizens.

Evidence is someone's support for his or her reasoning. Evidence can be a historical or current example, quotation from an expert, or statistics. Here are the completed versions of the arguments started above with the evidence also added.

- I am tired. There was so much noise by the neighbors last night that I only got three hours of sleep and I need at least eight hours to be fully rested. In fact, my personal doctor, Dr. Kennedy, even recommended that I try to get ten hours of sleep whenever possible to be fully rested.
- I like to travel. I enjoy meeting different people and visiting places that I could only imagine. The new people and experiences of travel help me realize how much I have to learn about the world, which helps motivate me to study. I recently met members of my family who had emigrated to Germany more than 20 years ago. They explained cultural differences in fashion, music, language, food, and education. It made me want to learn more about Germany and Europe, and they wanted to learn more about my life. We decided to write to each other each month to explore our differences and similarities.
- Diseases have serious economic costs. Diseases reduce the number of days that people are able to go to work. Sick people do not go to work. It also makes them less productive when they are at work. When people are ill, they do not work as quickly or as hard. Because diseases reduce work, there are not as many products made or customers served. According to a report from the U.S. National Institutes of Health in 2000, the annual economic cost of illness in the United States is $3 trillion. Diseases have a significant effect on the economy.

Refuting an argument

It is not enough to have arguments. It is also important to defeat any opposing arguments. The skill used to defeat the arguments of another person is called refutation. Refutation is the process of proving that a claim or argument is wrong. To prove that an argument is wrong, it is possible to challenge the reasoning on which it is based. It is possible to show that the argument is not well thought out or illogical. It is also possible to challenge the facts, the evidence, in different ways:

- It is possible to challenge the source of facts. Some information sources are not experts; they do not have the knowledge to have a meaningful opinion on a topic. For example, almost anyone can publish on the Internet. That makes it difficult to judge whether the information is accurate.
- Some sources of information have biases. Businesses that make a profit from genetic research are not likely to argue that "genetic research is a threat." This does not mean that those businesses cannot have something to say about genetic research. It might mean that it would be better to use a more unbiased source, or a range of sources, in making a decision about genetic research.

> *Student debate*

It is easy to understand the principles of argumentation, but more difficult to apply them. It takes practice. Regular participation in discussions and debates helps students learn the skills of effective public speaking, critical listening and thinking, argumentation, and refutation. Students learn to select the most significant and relevant issues, disprove the key issues of their opponents, and deliver speeches in a calm and confident style.

- Sometimes the information is not up-to-date. It is too old or events have changed. There are rapid technological advances in the field of genetics. Problems of the past may have been solved; new difficulties may have appeared.
- Finally, any evidence can be challenged with other expert opinion, counterexamples, and different statistics.

> *The double helix*

Cells carry the hereditary information they use to operate. A cell's DNA passes the cell's **traits**, its basic features, and its characteristics to the next generation. DNA stands for deoxyribonucleic acid. It is in the shape of a double helix, something like a twisted ladder. DNA has chemical instructions that pass the hereditary traits from parent to offspring for all living organisms. Genes are the sections of the DNA molecule that carry specific instructions, such as height, and hair and eye color. In 1953, James Watson and Francis Crick discovered the double helix structure for the DNA molecule. Their conclusions were based on X-ray images taken by Rosalind Franklin.

What Is Genetic Research?

Austrian priest Gregor Mendel (1822-1884) was the father of modern genetics. He studied changes in the plants that he was **cross-breeding** in the garden of his monastery. **Mendel's Laws** were the first on **heredity**, the study of inherited characteristics—the traits that are carried from parent to offspring. Although the importance of his research was not recognized for several decades, it was later used to begin the study of genetics. Genetic research is the study of genes and their functions for the purpose of understanding heredity. Genetic research includes DNA and **chromosome** analysis and testing. Researchers examine the changes, **variations**, and mutations of genes.

Billions of dollars are spent in biomedical genetic research each year to learn about the instructions that are carried in DNA that help make human beings and other animals. There is also genetic research which is used to produce crops that can resist pests, diseases, and drought. Many organizations, such as governments, medical and drug companies, research institutes and hospitals, and universities are involved in human genetic research. Genetic research is a key to the development of new drugs and medical procedures to improve health. Desire to improve human health is the basis for much of the world's financial investment in genetic research.

Genetic mutations

Scientists researching human genes carefully investigate areas about genetic instructions. They also study how the passing of characteristics from one generation to the next can go wrong. These errors are called **mutations**. They affect the inherited traits passed from one generation to the next. Mutations occur as traits are passed from a parent to an offspring. The result of a mutation is usually harmful, but might also be positive. Mutations can occur naturally, although they are not that common. Some mutations cause genetic diversity, producing new species of plants and animals. A mutation may also be caused by environmental factors. Radiation, for example, may change DNA, causing it to break its chemical bonds. This may produce new plant varieties or may lead to illnesses in humans or animals.

Human genetic research and health

According to the American Medical Association, biomedical researchers already know that there are more than 1,000 diseases with genetic causes. Genetic testing to prevent and treat disease is already an important part of human genetic research. This testing is now taking place throughout the world. Laboratories have made more than 900 different genetic tests available for use. But is it fair that some people could get tests and medical treatment to improve their health but others will not? Is it possible that the genetic study of human beings could be used for unethical purposes? Could it reveal something about a person's identity, family history, or medical problems which that person would prefer to keep private? What if a person discovered that she or he had a higher than normal risk of developing a serious disease—would that reduce the quality of life? Former British Prime Minister Tony Blair believed that there were both benefits and risks with genetic research:

> "We cannot resist change, but our job—indeed, our duty—is to make sense of change, to help people through it, to seize the massive opportunities for better health and better quality of life and then, with equal vigor, to minimize the threats such developments pose."
>
> [From a statement by Tony Blair on June 26, 2000]

Could genetic research be used by terrorists to make dangerous biological weapons, even **weapons of mass destruction**? Are there more benefits or more potential harms? What do you think?

Genetic research and crime

Because genetic research involves the examination and identification of plant and animal material, it has legal, national security, and other uses. For more than a decade, DNA analysis has been an important part of criminal investigations and prosecutions. Police officials have used DNA analysis to identify both criminals and crime victims. Forensic scientists, the people who collect, identify, and analyze physical evidence at a crime scene or for civil trials, use advances in genetic research to help locate and convict the guilty and free the innocent. The Innocence Project, for example, is an organization of lawyers, researchers, and community activists, which uses DNA evidence to help win the freedom of wrongfully convicted criminal defendants in the United States. More than 200 previously convicted individuals, including more than 40 defendants convicted of murder, have been released through careful examination of DNA evidence technology.

DNA evidence has been used to release innocent people from prison. But prosecutors in some places now use DNA evidence to keep people in prison for crimes for which they have not been tried. For example, some prisoners are ready to be released from prison after serving their sentences, but may be held because they are a "danger to society"—the proof of their dangerousness is DNA evidence at crime scenes. Should someone be held in prison based on DNA even when that evidence is not used in a criminal trial?

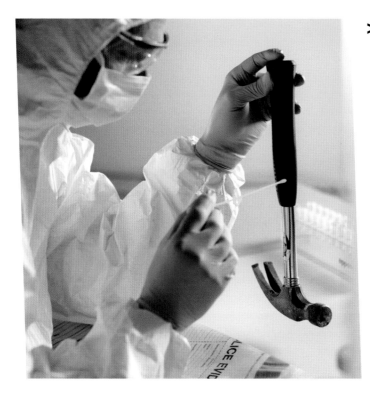

> **DNA evidence does solve crimes**

Modern technology, including DNA testing, has changed criminal investigations and prosecutions. It is possible to get at the truth and improve justice with DNA information, which might point to a specific person present during a crime.

Genetic research and agriculture

Did you know that according to the UN's Food and Agricultural Organization, more than 800 million people suffer from hunger and malnutrition? That oceans and rivers contain pollution and hazardous waste that come from the production of food? Businesses and governments are funding agricultural genetic research to come up with solutions to these challenging global problems. The U.S. Department of Agriculture reported that as much as one-third of the food supply in some countries is lost to plant viruses, weeds, and insect and animal pests. Genetic research is planned to improve the strength of plants, helping them to resist diseases and pests. Farmers now use pesticides to protect plants from insects and other pests, but these powerful poisons are often washed into nearby lakes and streams. Genetically improved plants may not need pesticides and other chemicals, which would reduce environmental pollution. In addition to research support for food production, there is genetic research designed to increase the health of the animals used in agriculture, such as dairy cattle, as well as to improve the production of nonfood agricultural goods, such as cotton.

 Can we feed the world?

In November 2001 the *International Treaty on Plant Genetic Resources for Food and Agriculture* stated:

"Plant genetic resources for food and agriculture are crucial in feeding the world's population. They are the raw material that farmers and plant breeders use to improve the quality and productivity of our crops. The future of agriculture depends on international cooperation and on the open exchange of the crops and their genes that farmers all over the world have developed and exchanged over 10,000 years. No country is sufficient in itself. All depend on crops and the genetic diversity within these crops from other countries and regions."

Genetic research and medical ethics

Whenever there is medical research and experimentation, there is a chance to develop new drugs and treatments that might improve the lives of millions of people. The history of genetic research includes careful work by responsible biomedical staffs, brilliant scientific breakthroughs, and applications of new ideas that have led to life-saving results. Medical research and human experimentation also has risks. Unfortunately, medical history reveals cases of sloppy laboratory work, fraud and falsified scientific research, and the manipulation of science for political purposes. Poor and prejudiced research can violate the privacy of patients. There have been notorious experiments in which hundreds of patients were infected with deadly diseases and then denied proper treatment. In the United States and the UK, prisoners, soldiers, the poor, and others have been infected with diseases and subjected to radiation for the purposes of research.

These are the potential benefits and costs of genetic research. Will it help us to understand the human body or will we know too much personal information about ourselves and others? Will it improve our health or harm it? Can we trust genetic researchers to behave **ethically**? The challenge is to carefully investigate the issues surrounding genetic research to find the right answers.

> *Tuskegee experiments*

From 1932, researchers for the U.S. Public Health Service infected hundreds of poor African Americans with the disease syphilis in order to examine the effects and some potential treatments for the disease. This took place in Tuskegee, Alabama. Many of the patients were denied effective medical treatment during the course of the study. The public outcry about these experiments encouraged governments and medical groups to establish principles for the ethical treatment of their patients.

Do the benefits outweigh the risks?

Genetic researches, particularly those using human subjects, are expected to carefully follow rules for the ethical treatment of their patients. If a scientist cr doctor violates these rules, as well as being morally questionable, it may cast doubt on the scientific conclusions of the research. In addition, the researcher may face criminal and civil penalties. Writer David Shenk weighs up some of the problems:

> "We're pursuing the human genome for good reasons, of course. With our new syllabus of genetic knowledge, we will become healthier and live longer. But even with the few facts that we now have, there is already cause to worry about the unintended consequences of acquiring such knowledge. If genes are the biological machine code—the software— containing the instructions for each person's development and decay, unlocking that code portends the ability to fix the bugs and even to add new features. When people worry aloud that we may soon be 'playing God,' it's because no living creature has ever before been able to upgrade its own operating system."
>
> [From a talk in 1997 by David Shenk (davidshenk.com), journalist and lecturer on education, health, and technology issues]

General ethical guide for genetic researchers

Here are some general practical ethics rules for genetic researchers. In this case, ethics rules means fair and safe behavior by doctors and medical researchers. Patients should agree to the research, be safe during any experiment, and be protected after the research has ended.

✔ Participation in research must be voluntary.
✔ Participation in research must be informed.
✔ The researcher must protect the privacy of the patient.
✔ The researcher must protect the privacy of others involved.
✔ The researcher must protect the biological materials used.
✔ The researcher must respect the welfare and safety of society.

Can you give a reason for each of these guidelines? Are there special rules that researchers should have for children? What do you think?

Organizations have different views on the value of genetic research. Science organizations prefer more research—they believe that it can be done effectively and for the good of all people. Some groups, for religious, cultural, economic, and social reasons, do not want to participate in genetic research and testing projects. If you wanted to persuade one of these groups to change their position on genetic research, how do you think you might do it?

For genetic research

"The discoveries made through these efforts will ultimately lead to profound advances in disease prevention and treatment. These are the kinds of innovative efforts that we should support. We must seize the historic opportunity provided by the Human Genome Project and the International HapMap Project, to speed up the discovery of the genetic causes of common diseases like diabetes and hypertension. At the same time, it's critical that we also understand the environmental contributors to sickness, and the interplay among genes and environment. There is not a moment to be lost."

[From a statement by Mike Leavitt, U.S. Secretary of Health and Human Services]

Against genetic research

"After careful review of the Human Genome Diversity Project, and other independent investigations on the genome of indigenous peoples, we find:
1. We declare absolute opposition to the Human Genome Diversity Project, and demand the immediate suspension of any activities to collect genetic samples, cell lines, or genetic data from indigenous peoples, including our deceased ancestors.
2. We demand the fullest cooperation of any government agency or independent research institute in the return of all genetic materials, cell lines, and data they may have in their possession to the appropriate governing authorities of the tribal group."

[A statement by the Indigenous Peoples Council on Biolcolonialism]

> *Genetic research lab safety precautions*

A level 4 bio-safety laboratory contains the most dangerous microorganisms. The scientists who perform the research and operate these labs require specific training. There is special equipment to contain any hazardous substances and reduce the threat to life. Because of the potential for producing highly dangerous diseases with genetic materials, some genetic research only takes place in these and other special labs.

How Do We Evaluate The Threat?

There will be substantial increases in genetic research and testing in the future. Governments are already spending additional millions of dollars on research programs. As the science of genetics advances, researchers will learn more about genes and what each one does. This will lead to the development of new technologies that take advantage of this new knowledge. For example, scientific breakthroughs in human genetic health may prevent or treat Huntington's and Alzheimer's disease, autism, diabetes, and sickle cell anemia. But no technology only has benefits. There are side-effects, unpredictable results, and risks. To make a decision about the threats of genetic research, it is important to consider and evaluate both the benefits and the risks.

To evaluate the threat of genetic research, a decision maker should be able to identify what is known and where there are gaps in knowledge. Without enough good quality information, it is difficult to decide if there should be more or less genetic research. In a study in the journal of the American Medical Association several years ago on the quality of genetic research, S. T. Bogardus, a health researcher, used seven different standards to test the quality of the research. More than 60 percent of the studies failed two or more of the standards. Do you think more and better research of this kind would help make the case for or against genetic research?

Has science moved too fast?

Scientists are usually careful in designing and recording experimental procedures. Their professional behavior is the beginning of serious evaluation of genetic research benefits and costs. The studies produced by scientists can be examined to make decisions about future promising research or the development of new medicines or technologies. However, as pointed up by these Spanish doctors, genetic research studies may not all be of high quality:

"The advances derived from the Human Genome Project have led to the development of new kinds of diagnostic tests, genetic, molecular or proteomic, which can be incorporated into clinical practice... The appearance of these new tests creates expectations, which often are not corroborated in clinical practice. This is due to the fact that sometimes the results of basic research are publicized without awaiting confirmation from the results of clinical research; at other times the clinical validation of the tests lacks **methodological** rigor, precisely for their having been developed in basic research environments without the collaboration of investigators with experience in clinical and **epidemiological** research... In genetic-molecular research, however, a single work analyzed the methodology of the studies published in four international medical journals, showing that 63% of them fulfilled only one of the required methodological criteria."

[From Drs. Lumbreras, Jarrin, and Aguado, Department of Public Health, University Miguel Hernandez, Alicante, Spain]

There are several questions that can be asked to help evaluate the risks of genetic research, such as:
• Who is involved in evaluating research?
• What should an evaluator do if the needed information is incomplete?
• What decision should be made to share the benefits of genetic research?
• How will research protect the natural environment?

More questions than answers

Can democratic principles help make the right decision? Who should make decisions regarding genetic science and technology policies? Should the decisions be left up to the experts, the scientists and doctors familiar with the technical issues of gene research? Should businesses funding the research, for example, pharmaceutical companies investigating genetics to produce new drugs, be involved in deciding which research is funded and who should receive the health benefits of the research? What about government? Many governments fund genetic research. They also have an interest in reducing health costs and protecting their citizens. Should they decide? What about individuals? After all, it is the person who will be tested and who will have to deal with the consequences. People themselves could be copied, manipulated, or changed through new genetic technologies. They might want to be involved in deciding the future of living organisms, including the human organism.

Each of these might have something to say about genetic research, but they might not agree about the research. Drug research for profit might not produce the medicines that are needed by the majority of people. Scientists might want to carry out as much research as possible while governments and individuals might want to restrict research for national security or privacy concerns. Who do you think should make the final decisions? Why?

Is it more likely that open public debate and discussion will help evaluate the benefits and risks of research? Or, is it more likely that constant debate will slow the introduction of necessary research that is vital to solving health and other problems?

> *There are potential risks*

Genetic research might provide public health benefits, but poorly controlled biological research could produce genetically based illnesses or pollution that would threaten large populations. These children in Asia are wearing masks for protection against infectious disease.

Using the precautionary principle

What should an evaluator do if the needed information is incomplete? If an action could cause harm, or the result of an experiment could be wildly unpredictable, then it might be better to be safe than sorry, better to be cautious than rush forward with a new idea. This is the precautionary principle. When the health of people or the environment might be in danger, a good decision maker would try to reduce the potential for harm. This might mean that those in favor of new technologies, such as the results of genetic research, would have the burden of proving that there would be little risk to society and the environment from their use.

The precautionary principle has risks. It might slow the pace of genetic research. Because it is difficult, if not impossible, to show that a technology has no risk, the principle might reduce the likelihood that the benefits of gene research would quickly go to those who need them. Nevertheless, the precautionary principle makes it less likely that a catastrophic or irreversible genetic problem would come from new research. What do you think is more important—Is it better to quickly help people in need with rapid research or is a slower and safer approach best?

Support for the precautionary principle

The Science and Environmental Health Network (SEHN) is trying to apply the precautionary principle to any policy that would affect the environment or public health:

"When an activity raises threats of harm to human health or the environment, precautionary measures should be taken even if some cause and effect relationships are not fully established scientifically. In this context the proponent of an activity, rather than the public, should bear the burden of proof. The process of applying the precautionary principle must be open, informed and democratic and must include potentially affected parties. It must also involve an examination of the full range of alternatives, including no action."

[From the SEHN Statement on the Precautionary Principle, January 1998]

How can decisions be made to share fairly the benefits of genetic research?

One of the most important considerations of genetic research and engineering is the distribution of the technologies, medicines, and other good results. Should the benefits be equally shared? If there is a genetic cure for diabetes, should it be made available to all? Should anyone be able to take advantage of the results if everyone cannot benefit? Should the poor have to wait until they can afford the medical drugs and agricultural technologies developed through genetic research? Is it fair if the research subjects are left out of the benefits of research? If research on HIV/AIDS is done on African people, should African countries be first on the list to receive those medicines?

This fair distribution of the benefits of genetic and advanced research and technology has been a problem. Wealthier countries and people can pay more for new technologies; they outbid many people who need but cannot afford new, often lifesaving, products. In the 30 years of Green Revolution at the end of the 20th century, new agricultural technologies used in Southeast Asia increased food crop production 114 percent. During the same time, hunger in that region increased 11 percent. Although the region used modified crops to produce more food, it was bought for a higher price by wealthier countries.

> Norman Borlaug

Norman Borlaug is an agricultural researcher and plant geneticist whose discoveries helped significantly increase the world food supply. Known as the "father of the Green Revolution," he was awarded the Nobel Peace Prize in 1970 for his efforts to reduce starvation in Asia and Africa.

The case of Harrison Bergeron

In American novelist Kurt Vonnegut's short story, "Harrison Bergeron," the author describes a world with the goal of perfect individual equality. The government handicaps the gifted, talented, and strong to reduce their skills to make them equal to those who are intellectually and physically weaker:

"THE YEAR WAS 2081, and everybody was finally equal. They weren't only equal before God and the law. They were equal every which way. Nobody was smarter than anybody else. Nobody was better looking than anybody else. Nobody was stronger or quicker than anybody else. All this equality was due to the 211th, 212th, and 213th Amendments to the Constitution, and to the unceasing vigilance of agents of the United States Handicapper General.

Some things about living still weren't quite right, though. April, for instance, still drove people crazy by not being springtime. And it was in that clammy month that the H-G men took George and Hazel Bergeron's fourteen-year-old son, Harrison, away.

It was tragic, all right, but George and Hazel couldn't think about it very hard. Hazel had a perfectly average intelligence, which meant she couldn't think about anything except in short bursts. And George, while his intelligence was way above normal, had a little mental handicap radio in his ear. He was required by law to wear it at all times. It was tuned to a government transmitter. Every twenty seconds or so, the transmitter would send out some sharp noise to keep people like George from taking unfair advantage of their brains."

[From the Kurt Vonnegut short story "Harrison Bergeron" in *Welcome to the Monkey House*. New York: Dell Publishing, 1973]

Do you think that the government should use genetic research to make people more equal, more exactly the same? Do you think it is fair for some people to get the benefits of genetic research when others do not? How would you make its use more fair?

How will research protect biodiversity?

Human activity, such as urban development and clearing the rain forest for timber and agriculture, has had a powerful and negative effect on **biodiversity**. The World Conservation Union estimates that plant and animal species curently are being eliminated 100 to 1,000 times faster than they would be in a natural environment. Many scientists argue that genetic research could work to sustain and build a diverse ecosystem. But the results of some research, such as agricultural research, have reduced diversity. At the beginning of the 20th century, there were tens of thousands of varieties of Asian rice. One hundred years later, there are only eight commonly grown. This is the result of monoculture, the use of a single genetic plant strain. New rice strains may be stronger species, but a single virus might also produce widespread crop failure.

✔ Making up your mind

A particularly careful person, when deciding about the threat of genetic research, might take into account:
✔ if the research seems to be done in an open and democratic way
✔ if caution has been used
✔ if the benefits are likely to be fairly shared
✔ if research will be done without hurting the natural environment.

This type of research is more likely to produce safe and effective results. But this sort of extraordinarily careful research takes time. During that additional time, it is possible that hundreds of thousands of individuals will face disabling and life-threatening diseases, the food supply will be at risk, and species will become extinct. If you had to make the decision to fund genetic research, what would you do? Would you try to get immediate benefits or would you be more cautious?

> Biodiversity preserves the natural environment
Life thrives in a biologically varied environment. Different plant and animal species and microorganisms each play an important role in maintaining and preserving the environment. Can genetic research put this variety at risk?

> *Will genetic research lead to designer babies?*

"*Custom-designed… Attractive features… Just the right color, tone, weight, and style…*" Is this an advertisement for a new model of car or for a genetically enhanced child? Technological advances in gene research and engineering may soon lead to options for planning a child in ways that parents never could have previously imagined.

Genetic Research For The Individual And Society

In 1952, genetic scientists **cloned** the first animal, a tadpole. A clone is a genetically identical copy of another living creature. There are naturally occurring genetic copies such as identical twins. But it was an extraordinary achievement for scientists to produce an exact genetic copy, with matching DNA. Since that time, researchers have cloned many animals.

Because genetic research can change the building blocks of life, it has important consequences for individuals and societies. One day, perhaps, scientists will have the skills to clone a part or all of a human being. Will that change the way people think of themselves? Patients who have a heart or liver transplant may feel differently about their experience. A cardiac transplant support group member recalls, "I know I wouldn't be here if I didn't have that heart. In a way it's like I am living someone else's life. They say recipients will have heart transplant tendencies—you take on some of the characteristics of the donor."

Will people feel less than unique if a genetic copy can be made? What about the person who has received gene therapy to become taller, stronger, or more intelligent? Is there a risk that person will feel more than human? Is a genetically improved person better than others? If you were much bigger, stronger, and taller than others, would you feel that you were a better person?

Genetic research and sport

Some athletes, driven by a fierce competitive spirit, desire for fame and glory, or the financial rewards from sport, take illegal and unethical shortcuts. They cheat. This has happened without the benefit of genetic research, but medical advances may make it more difficult to find and stop the cheating athlete.

Marion Jones, one of the stars of the 2000 Summer Olympic Games, won five track and field medals. In 2007, she confessed that she had cheated; she had taken steroids to boost her performance prior to that Olympics. She was ordered to return her three gold and two bronze medals. Floyd Landis was stripped of the championship of the world's most famous cycling event, the Tour de France, when he tested positive for a banned performance-enhancing drug.

What might happen in the world of sport and athletics if individuals could manipulate their genetic background to be taller, faster, or have better hand-eye coordination? What if a person could be designed to match the physical needs of a sport? The same research that might improve general public health could assist athletes. Individuals suffering from many diseases have a loss of muscle strength. Those with asthma have reduced lung capacity. Genetic research to help with the symptoms of these and other illnesses may also lead scientists to discover how to add muscle mass to rugby and football players, increase the oxygen capacity of long-distance runners and swimmers, and reduce the time that it takes to recover from a sport injury.

The International Olympic Committee and the World Anti-Doping Agency (WADA) now ban the participation of genetically modified athletes:

"The International Olympics Committee (IOC) and the World Anti-Doping Agency have decided to add human genetic modification to their list of banned practices. Effective January 1, 2003, 'Gene or cell doping is defined as the non-therapeutic use of genes, genetic elements, and/or cells that have the capacity to enhance athletic performance.'

In the past, WADA has been forced to react as new drugs have been developed and used... By introducing the notion of genetic doping into the list at this time, we are taking into account the important changes occurring in doping techniques."

> *Can genetic research create better athletes?*

Some professional sports organizations actively promote genetic research. For example, the British Association of Sport and Exercise Sciences has called for more genetic research into the sports and exercise sciences because of the anticipated benefits for public health, but want researchers to take a more active role in debating the implications of their work with the public. "If a powerful muscle growth gene was identified, on the one hand this could help develop training programs that increase muscle size and strength in athletes, but even more importantly, the knowledge could be used to develop exercise programs or drugs to combat muscle wasting in old age," said Dr. Alun Williams from England's Manchester Metropolitan University, one of the report's authors.

Should genetic enhancement of athletes be allowed?

Do you think performance-enhancing medical procedures, including genetic research-based improvements, should be legalized for athletes? What if cheaters cannot be identified and stopped? A 2004 *Science News* article reported: "... scientists are increasingly concerned that sophisticated techniques for evading drug tests will make it difficult for testers to catch athletes using steroids and other drugs, especially at future athletic competitions when genetic-based enhancements are expected to be prevalent."

Will sports authorities end up having to accept genetic changes that enhance performances because they cannot stop them? What do you think?

Cloning

Cloning is the creation of a genetically identical copy of a living thing. Some simple organisms who reproduce asexually (without a partner of the opposite sex) do this every time they reproduce. Now, scientists have the knowledge and technological skills to clone more advanced living things.

✔ Types of cloning

Reproductive cloning – This is a method to make an exact genetic copy, to produce a new animal, for example, which has the same DNA as a previous animal. In 1996, Dolly, a sheep, was successfully cloned this way. About 90% or more of reproductive cloning experiments end in failure. Dolly was a successful clone but she was one of 277 tries to clone a sheep. The film, *Jurassic Park*, is the story of using reproductive cloning to produce extinct dinosaurs. Today scientists are using reproductive cloning to protect endangered species; they may use the technology to reproduce a previously extinct species in the future. In Italy in 2001, for example, geneticists successfully cloned a mouflon, an endangered wild sheep. Chinese scientists have stored the DNA of the giant panda to guarantee its survival.

DNA/gene cloning – This procedure makes copies of a gene in order to produce material for future study. This is valuable lab work, because scientists would like to have a supply of identical material for more accurate testing. DNA cloning is the least controversial of the different types of cloning.

Therapeutic cloning– This is the treatment of illness or injury. Therapeutic cloning involves the use of human embryos and other human materials in medical research. Scientists use this method to study different medical procedures to attempt to prevent or treat heart disease, cancer, Alzheimer's, and diabetes. They might also produce organs, such as kidneys, livers, and lungs, for the hundreds of thousands of patients needing organ transplants.

Think about it!

Many people do not support human cloning. It is controversial because of religious or moral concerns—cloning may be "playing God." Others worry about producing people with superior, or superhuman, traits. Some governments have already banned it; others are planning to outlaw it. What is your opinion on human cloning? Could you defend a new opinion from another person's perspective? How would your opinion change, if at all, if you were faced with any of the following situations?
- You have a disease and would benefit from therapeutic cloning.
- You have lost a relative in a tragic accident and want a clone of them.

- You are a geneticist doing human health research and need cloned material.
- You are a clone.

Family history

Genetic research can help individuals discover their personal and family history. It can also aid researchers, historians, geographers, archaeologists, teachers, and students to learn about human history. Based on DNA testing from different regions of the world, some geneticists have made the claim that all humans on Earth have a common ancestor—a woman who lived in Africa up to 200,000 years ago. Using the data from this research, scientists may also learn the path of human migration from one part of the world to another. Individuals are also paying for personal DNA history results, to identify their own ancestry.

✔ Bioarchaeology

Imagine that you have been told for your entire life that you were of 100% African descent. What would you think if DNA testing revealed that was not true? How would you think about yourself? Would you worry about a loss of identity or would you be eager to find out about your new identity? DNA testing can lead to many dilemmas.

> *Cloning livestock and endangered animals*

Most of cloning research has been done with animals. Farmers and ranchers could use cloning technology to speed up the reproduction of their healthiest animals. Zoologists and some environmentalists want to have cloning available to reproduce endangered or even extinct species.

> *Forensic science*

Forensic science involves the gathering and analysis of
evidence. This may occur at a crime scene, or in later stages of
a criminal investigation. Forensic science is also used in civil
trials. A significant and increasing part of forensic science is
genetic testing, leading to the use of DNA evidence in trials.

Genetic Research, Crime, And The Law

With the exception of identical twins, each person has unique DNA. DNA can be found in all body parts, in tissue and fluids, bones, teeth, skin, hair, blood, and saliva. People leave their DNA wherever they travel and whatever they do. Skin cells and hair are shed on the ground, in cars and public transportation, and on clothing. Saliva is present on envelopes, stamps, restaurant utensils, and chewing gum. Because DNA can identify a particular person and, if a person is present, their DNA can generally be found, police investigators, private detectives, national security agents, counterterrorism forces, and others have shown great interest in DNA. New research and technologies are making it easier to use.

In the early 1980s, medical technicians and doctors performing examinations of murder victims noticed that the killers often left DNA evidence. At the time, genetic research and testing was not good enough to regularly use this information to find or prosecute the criminals. During the next decade, the advances in genetic testing made it possible to use DNA evidence in courts of law. There was an explosion of this evidence in the 1990s—more than 20,000 criminal trials in the United States had included DNA evidence by 2000.

DNA support for law enforcement

DNA evidence can assist the police in criminal investigations. It lets the police know who might have been present at a crime scene as a witness or criminal. It helps identify missing persons and bodies that are in a condition that they cannot otherwise be identified. Of equal importance, DNA evidence can let the police and defense lawyers know who was not at a crime scene. It can protect the innocent.

Identification

Criminal identification is a difficult business. Although people are likely to believe that they have an accurate memory of events, eyewitness testimony is often mistaken. The shock of witnessing a crime interferes with eyewitness identifications; memory fades over time. Psychology professors Brian Cutler and Steven Penrod concluded that in the United States, there may be as many as 5,000 wrongful convictions based on eyewitness testimony each year. The use of DNA evidence may add to or substitute for inaccurate testimony, such as that from an eyewitness. This makes it more likely that the real criminal will go to prison. DNA evidence can also be used to overturn wrongful convictions. The Innocence Project, an organization that uses genetic information to help people serving prison sentences, has freed more than 200 innocent criminal defendants in the United States.

Genetic databases

Countries are interested in gathering information on criminals to help protect society from those people who will commit future crimes. Government officials know that people who have a criminal history are more likely to commit crimes in the future. This is called recidivism—the repetition of criminal behavior. In the United States, 60 percent of criminals return to prison after their release. In the United Kingdom, it is 50 percent. In Australia it's 40 percent. Police forces would like effective tools to quickly track down these criminals. This is one reason that many countries are developing genetic databases, collections of DNA information on criminals.

DNA criminal databases are controversial. In the United States, different states have different databases. Because they are not linked together, they are less effective than a national database. Some states allow the information to be used for medical research, which can be argued violates the privacy of those in the database. In the United Kingdom, individuals can have their DNA included in the database if they have been arrested, even if they are not convicted of a crime. In fact, it is possible for a person to have their DNA included in the national database even if they are never charged with a crime. DNA evidence can be held as long as the UK government wants to keep it. This means that the government may hold genetic information despite a person's innocence.

How would you regulate a national DNA crime database?

Imagine that you were the director of a national DNA database. What decision would you make about each of the following issues?

✔ Should the database include those arrested for a crime, those convicted of a crime, or everyone?

✔ Should the information be used just for crime control or should it be used for other purposes, like health research?

✔ Should there be DNA testing for every trial, to make sure that the criminal defendant is not wrongfully convicted?

> *Eyewitness identification – is it accurate enough?*

Police frequently use eyewitnesses to identify criminal suspects, such as the fictional lineup shown here. Most jurors believe the testimony of eyewitnesses, but studies show that their testimony is often wrong. DNA can provide much more accurate results.

Genetic research and predicting future behavior

Medical professionals use more than 1,200 genetic tests to identify potential disorders and illnesses. New genetic research has shown, however, that up to half of human behavioral problems, including depression, anxiety, and violence, may have genetic causes. There is increasing interest in these issues, which might be used to predict and treat the potential dangerousness of a person. The Youth Violence Initiative, a project by the U.S. National Institute of Mental Health, was designed to identify youth with a high risk of participating in future criminal conduct. Once identified, often by examining genetic codes that would be related to future violence or criminal behavior, those individuals could be subject to medical treatment, often through the use of prescribed drugs. This may potentially violate the civil liberties of youth because they would be given treatment, not for their criminal conduct, but their potential for criminal conduct. It is a very controversial application of genetic information. Do you think that genetic research should be used to predict and treat people who are more likely to have traits for future aggression, anger, or depression?

> *Predicting future genetic harms*

The new world of genetic testing is raising troubling issues about how people should predict and plan for the future. Genetic testing may show that some people have a good chance of suffering from a particular genetic disorder or illness. If there is a genetic threat to an embryo that is made worse by the environment in a workplace, should a pregnant woman lose her job? If she continues to work, should she face criminal charges for neglect or abuse for any later health problems her child has? The pregnant woman shown here is working on a construction site.

Genetic research and addiction

As genetic research becomes more effective, and the secrets of genes are unlocked, will a government "treat" people for their addiction to alcohol, drugs, or cigarettes even before they begin using those substances? Will governments and mental health officials want to isolate or treat the hundreds of thousands of people who might later suffer from depression? Civil rights supporters are concerned about the amount of control that a government might use to reduce the social problems that could be identified by genetic research and testing.

What about businesses? Could they limit opportunities for workers who might have genetic disorders or illnesses? Could they require genetic tests for employees? Businesses want to make a profit. As worker costs increase, profits decrease. Businesses want to cut their costs. In the future, more businesses may use this as a reason to require genetic tests for workers. Businesses will want to know if workers are likely to get sick or retire early due to poor health. They may not want to hire people likely to have addictive personalities or who are criminal risks. Although laws in some places protect workers from some forms of genetic discrimination, few countries have laws in place to give full protection. Should laws be changed to protect people from any form of genetic discrimination?

> *Can the genetic code break the cycle of addiction?*

The genetic code of an individual may show a risk for addictive behavior, such as alcoholism, gambling, or smoking. This would be valuable information for someone to have. The person could then avoid the addiction or seek counseling or treatment. This kind of information about an individual's future may be more threatening when it is in the hands of the government, which might take more serious actions to stop future addiction, mental illness, or crime.

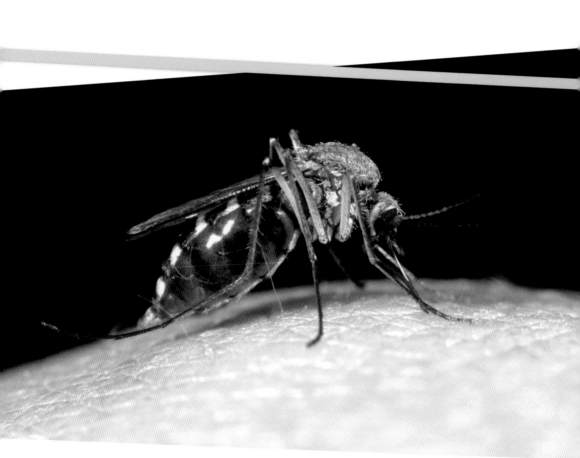

> *Genetic research discovers treatments for life-threatening diseases*

Malaria is one of the world's deadliest diseases. Caused by a parasite, 300-500 million people become sick each year, with more than one million dying, mostly children. There is no effective vaccine and treatment does not always work. Geneticists have made progress examining the parasite that causes the illness and may be able to figure out the way it resists medical treatment.

Genetic Research And Health

Genetic research is being used to improve understanding about the way individual genes and groups of genes influence human health. By identifying the genetic factors that cause disease or prevent the body from healing, it will be easier for biotechnology companies to make more effective drugs. It will be simpler for doctors to prevent, diagnose, and treat illnesses.

Individuals also have a role to play. Family medical history is an important part of the cycle of disease. Genetic traits that increase the likelihood of specific illnesses are often passed on from one generation to the next, from the parent to the child. A family medical history that includes heart disease, cystic fibrosis, cancer, sickle cell anemia, or diabetes might increase the risk of those in later generations. In a survey by the office of the U.S. Surgeon General, more than 90 percent of Americans thought that it was important to know family medical history to improve their health. But only 33 percent had tried to collect information to make such a history. There is now online U.S. government assistance, the Family History Initiative, to help everyone learn about the connection between heredity and disease in order to prepare for a healthier future. More personal genetic information may help make individuals healthier.

Genetic research and inherited diseases

Genetic testing has obvious benefits—it helps diagnose illnesses for prevention or early treatment. Doctors have more opportunities to improve health if they can identify and treat an illness at the earliest possible time. Some people tested for genetic health disorders are already sick. But others are healthy. They are tested because they are at risk of developing an illness later in life. They might even receive treatment—drugs or surgery—to prevent a future disease that might never develop. This "cure for the healthy" is very controversial. Not only does it use medical resources for people when they are healthy, it could also use medical treatments that might harm them.

> Is gene therapy an option for illnesses that affect the elderly?

As the population ages, more people are affected by Alzheimer's and Parkinson's disease, as well as by arthritis. Tens of millions of people may get relief from scientific breakthroughs in biotechnology into these conditions.

In testing for genetic disorders, lab workers examine the DNA, looking for clues that might increase the risk of one or more diseases in a patient. In fact, there are 4,000 diseases, such as Tay Sachs, sickle cell anemia, and hemophilia, which are caused by a single mutation in a single gene. Genetic tests are now available for use on embryos and infants, as well as on adults for diseases that might happen later in life, like Alzheimer's and various forms of cancer.

Organ donation and xenotransplantation

Dozens of people die each day while they wait for human donors. Kidneys, livers, lungs, and hearts for transplantation are in short supply. Thousands more are needed. In the future, biotechnologists may be able to produce human donor organs in a laboratory. With genetic engineering, the new organ may be grown from the patient's own tissue, making it unlikely that his or her immune system would reject the organ when it is surgically placed in the body. In addition, scientists may be able to produce hearts and kidneys in genetically altered pigs, also reducing the chance of the human body rejecting the donated organ.

The use of an organ transplanted from one species into another is called **xenotransplantation**. Xenotransplantation may provide hope for thousands of people who need new organs, but it also has significant risks. Genetic modification of animals, or transplantation of organs, may make it easier for viruses and parasites to move from one species to another. Illnesses that have never before affected human beings could spread through large populations with disastrous results.

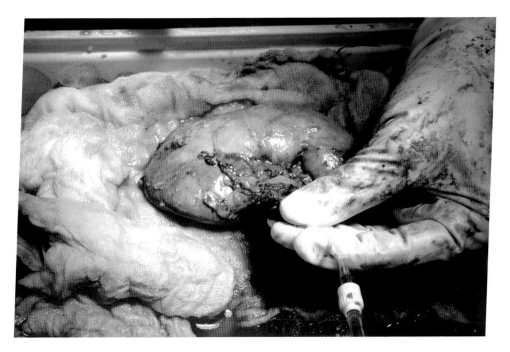

> *Global organ shortage*

There is a shortage of human organs for transplant patients. The available supply only meets ten percent of the need. In the future, therapeutic cloning could help produce hundreds of thousands of livers, kidneys, and hearts for transplant.

Improved medical treatment

DNA research might improve the quality of current medical care. Millions of people worldwide suffer from serious health effects each year because they have a negative or allergic reaction to prescription drugs. Hundreds of thousands of them die. For example, the Institute of Medicine reported in 2000 that there are two million cases of negative drug reactions in the United States each year, and more than 100,000 people die as a result. It is the fourth leading cause of death, ahead of AIDS, diabetes, and accidents.

Genetic research might be able to produce technologies that would match prescription drugs to the individual DNA of a patient. This would decrease the chance that a patient would have an allergic or other reaction to the medicine. Scientists may also discover the genetic reasons for why a treatment that works for two-thirds of patients is ineffective or deadly for the other third. This would help scientists to test or engineer genes to improve healing. It would also give doctors the information that they need to select the best possible medical treatment.

 Think differently

Many of the lab techniques for DNA testing involve the use of experimental animals. Animals are modified genetically to test particular genes—mice have been made to "glow in the dark." Biotechnologists have to consider using animals, like pigs and cows, to grow and harvest human organs. Gene cloning also creates an opportunity to reduce animal testing.

✔ Should animals be used in scientific testing?
✔ Is it cruel to use them to produce vaccines or body parts for human medical treatments?
✔ Is research testing on animals different from hunting animals or using them for food?
✔ If there are alternatives to animal tests, but they are much more expensive, should we pay extra to protect animals?

Risks and benefits

Research on any biological materials, particularly the sources of life and health, has the potential for great benefits. It also carries great challenges and risks. Even if research is done for a good purpose, it could backfire. What do you think of the decision to use reverse genetic engineering to produce one of the deadliest diseases of the 20th century, the 1918 Spanish flu, which killed more than 20 million people? Here are two opinions:

> *Biological agents are weapons of mass destruction*

Genetic research for human health studies the bacteria and viruses that cause serious illness. This same research could be used to make or deliver genetic weapons, a form of biological warfare that might be a global threat to health.

"For the first time, this deadly 1918 Spanish flu virus has been reconstructed and characterized... Their goal is to gain a greater understanding of this virus in order to use this knowledge to predict future pandemics and develop novel vaccines and treatments... This research is one example of the potential ability of researchers to answer important disease questions, long unsolvable, until the recent and successful sequencing of varied microbial and cellular genomes. Studies can now be safely conducted on genes and their components that were not possible in previous times due to these advances and progress in the genetic manipulation of viruses."

[From *News-Medical.Net*, October 2005]

"A resuscitation of the Spanish flu is neither necessary nor warranted from a public health point of view... But there is little need for antiviral drugs against the 1918 strain if the 1918 strain had not been recreated in the first place. 'It simply does not make any scientific sense to create a new threat just to develop new countermeasures against it,' said Jan van Aken, biologist with the Sunshine Project. 'Genetic characterization of influenza strains has important biomedical applications. But it is not justifiable to recreate this particularly dangerous eradicated strain that could wreak havoc if released, deliberately or accidentally,' he added."

[Source: The Sunshine Project, 2005]

> *Monocultural agricultural development*

Monoculture is the use of a single crop in an area. Although it does not have the benefit of biodiversity, many agricultural specialists prefer the use of a single and stronger crop variety. If a plant can be engineered to resist drought, cold weather, insects, and weeds, it might produce more food than traditional, diverse seeds and plants. The danger is that the plants have the same biology—a disease or pest that affects one plant might destroy an entire crop.

Genetic Research And Nonhuman Life

Governments and businesses have a strong incentive to increase their support for plant and animal genetic research. Governments are responsible for their people. They need to provide the basics of human life. Genetic research has the possibility of increasing food supplies, as well as developing technologies to produce more fresh water, reduce pollution, and improve health.

Businesses want to make a profit. Genetic research, testing, and engineering are growing industries. Billions of dollars are spent each year in biotechnology to promote new foods, industrial agricultural products, and medicines.

There are enormous fortunes to be made with the next generation of scientific advances. If research is done in a thoughtful and careful way, the results ought to help increase knowledge and understanding about the design and evolution of life. If the research is of poor quality or risky, then the long-term results may be disastrous.

Is it right for genes to be patented?

A patent is a legal agreement between a government and an inventor. It allows an inventor to be the only person who can make or receive money for the invention for a period of time. Some countries, such as the United States, have let businesses and scientists get patents for genetically modified plants and animals. Patents protect inventors, so no one can steal their ideas and use them without paying the inventors for their work. Patents have also allowed companies to invest in research, hoping to gain financial rewards later. But patents also interfere with research and development.

Scientists and businesses that are involved in genetic research want to get the financial rewards of their work. They often work in secret, making sure that no one knows anything about their research until they are able to file for a patent and get complete control over the invention. This means that they do not work with other scientists, publish their research, attend scientific meetings, or discuss breakthroughs. Because there is less scientific cooperation, the research results are more likely to be of lower quality when they are finally known. Secrecy can also delay the research or slow technologies getting to the market, so that people needing them will not get them as quickly as they would like.

> **Genetic engineering might help clean up the planet**

Genetic research on plants and microorganisms could reduce the effects of pollution. Bacteria are known to break down pesticides and other toxic pollution. If scientists could discover the genes that do it, they might be able to produce bacteria to clean hazardous waste sites or oil spills.

✔ What do they think?

Without private profit, there would be less genetic research:

"Taking away incentives may cause research to become a largely publicly funded activity, guided (or stifled) by the mores (and agenda) of the incumbent government and subject to political approvals. Privatization of research allows greater independence from political intervention. In defense of private companies it is said that the desire to make profits is not devoid of reasoning. Logic dictates that products must be priced at an affordable price for profits to be realized…In summary, the present incentive is for researchers to patent sequences or partial sequences of human genes. Further, the focus of substantive research has become profit driven."

Prof. D. du Toit, Professor of Health Sciences, Tshwane University of Technology, South Africa, 2006

Patents reduce gene research and testing:

"Gene patents can interfere with clinical adoption of genetic tests, potentially compromising the quality of testing by limiting the development of higher quality and lower-cost alternative testing methods. A survey of 72 genetic-testing laboratories found that 25 percent of the laboratories have been deterred from offering a test due to the enforcement of a patent or license."

Lori Andrews and Jordan Paradise, Yale Journal of Health Policy, Law and Ethics, 2005

> **Genetic engineering may preserve Earth's biological heritage**

Thousands of animal and plant species have been eliminated or are endangered due to human activity, according to Dr. Paul Ehrlich (shown here), President of the Center for Conservation Biology at Stanford University. The clearing of forests, pollution of the air and water, and city and population growth have reduced the natural habitat for many living organisms. Genetic engineering may offer the hope that these species could be restored or preserved. The ability to preserve species in a lab might also mean that some people will not think there is a reason to save them in the wild.

Trade secrets

Businesses can protect their private information. This is called a trade secret. It makes sense that a business would not want to share its strategies and product information with competitors. One problem is that it also hides information from the public. There have been hundreds of experiments with genetically modified organisms, but it is difficult to know which plants or animals are affected or what the health or environmental risks to consumers might be because the information can be protected as a trade secret.

GMOs

The use of genetically modified organisms (GMOs) in agriculture is one of the most controversial issues in the field of genetic research and engineering. Some countries have quite a lot of GMOs in agriculture and the food supply. In the United States, more than 3,000 genetically modified plants, animals, and microorganisms have been tested. Some countries, such as France, Austria, and Greece, have banned a number of these products. Others have taken a middle ground, marking GMOs so that consumers can make their own decisions about what to use. In December 2007, France and Germany made different decisions on the same genetically modified corn crop on the same day. According to *Planet Ark News*:

> "Germany lifted its own ban on use of the MON 810 technology on the day France announced its suspension. Germany's move came after Monsanto agreed to additional monitoring of its use."

✔ Think about it

Is it right to worry about GMOs? What do you think should be done about them?
✔ Should they be banned?
✔ Should we be told where GM crops are growing?
✔ Should products have labels which identify genetically modified ingredients?
✔ Should GMOs be tested and then encouraged if found to be safe?

One thing is clear. Serious debate on the ethical, social, political, and scientific issues of genetic research is needed to make better and more informed decisions about lifesaving or potentially risky tests and treatments. Because of this, organizations reviewing genetic research have, from the start, called for more education and debate:

"The results from human genome research is being used to develop treatments for genetic disorders; some actually correcting the adverse mutations of the sufferer's DNA. New gene-based or gene-directed methods, including gene therapy, are currently being developed for treating conditions such as cystic fibrosis and adenosine deaminase (ADA) deficiency. Such applications, while still in their early stages, are likely to grow. The early developments in human genome research are promising, but at the same time they have raised questions concerning safety, ethical, social, legal and economic issues, extending to the debate about patents concerning human DNA ... At the national level, several countries have established committees whose activities include encouraging public debate, improving public education, developing advice or guidelines, and linking with their respective parliaments."

[European Federation of Biotechnology, *Report on the Application of Human Genetic Research*, 1995]

> ### Developing new animals—the Labradoodle dog

In the 1980s, an Australian created a new hybrid dog breed from two pure bred dogs. He crossed a Labrador retriever and a standard poodle to make the Labradoodle. The Labradoodle later gained fame when professional golfer Tiger Woods became an owner.

Join the debate on genetic research

Now you've had a chance to read lots of evidence on both sides of the genetic research story. It's time to try to use that knowledge in a debate or argument.

Speaking skills

Good communication skills will help you succeed in debates and classroom discussions and improve relationships with family and friends. Effective public speakers are able to meet new people, speak in a confident manner, organize presentations, participate in serious class and community discussions on important topics, and respect the opinions of others. Persuasive public speakers have the right mix of reasoned arguments and emotional appeals to impress the majority of listeners. They speak with enough volume and emphasis and use eye contact and gestures to connect with an audience. Good speakers research and know their topics, practice their delivery, and anticipate the argument challenges from an opponent or difficult question from a member of the audience. They may use many of the same techniques, but there is no one best way to deliver a speech.

Kinds of debates

- *Formal debate.* The most popular debating model is to have two sides arguing for and against a specific topic. One side makes a case for the topic and the other disagrees. Any number of students, but usually two or three, is on each side.
- *Discussion format.* A group of students participates in a panel discussion on an issue. Students speak for themselves and may agree or disagree with the opinions of others on the panel. There is an overall time limit, for example, 30 minutes. You can use a moderator to ask questions. Audience questions may be added after the discussion.
- *Open forum.* This is an effective format for a class or large group. A single **moderator** leads an open discussion on a range of topics. Members of the audience may present new ideas, add to the presentations from others, or refute any issue. The event may last for an hour or more.

Organizing a debate or discussion

Each format has a particular set of rules. You can change rules for the number or participants or amount of time you have available for an event. In a formal debate, one side makes a case for the topic. The other side argues against the case. The side arguing for the topic is called the proposition; the other side is called the opposition. Each speaker on a side delivers a speech. The teams alternate speakers. The proposition team, which must prove that the topic is more likely to be true, speaks first and last. The first opposition speaker refutes the case. Second speakers continue with their team's points and refute new points from the other side. The final speeches are summaries of the best arguments for a team.

Speakers in a debate

✔ First speaker, proposition – 5 minutes
✔ First speaker, opposition – 5 minutes
✔ Second speaker, proposition – 5 minutes
✔ Second speaker, opposition – 5 minutes
✔ Third speaker, opposition – 3 minutes
✔ Third speaker, proposition – 3 minutes

It is possible to add a question and comment time by the opposing side or a class or audience during, in between, or after the speeches. An individual or group can judge a debate, voting on the outcome, but the votes must be for side that did the better job of debating. Judges should not simply vote for their personal opinion on the topic. Did the proposition proved the case or was the opposition able to defeat the proposition's arguments?

So, is genetic research a threat or not? What do you think?

> *Put your case forward effectively*

Genetic research is supported by governments, businesses, and scientific researchers. But there are also powerful opposition groups who want to regulate, limit, or even ban some or all kinds of genetic research. Debators presenting these issues must be effective speakers, with clever argument skills, to convince an audience that their opinion is the better one.

Find Out More

Glossaries

Diving into the Gene Pool—The Exploratorium Museum, San Francisco
http://www.exploratorium.edu/genepool/glossary.html

Genome Glossary—NOVA
http://www.pbs.org/wgbh/nova/genome/glossary.html

Genome Glossary—Human Genome Project
http://www.ornl.gov/sci/techresources/Human_Genome/glossary/

Genetic Glossary—CNN
http://www.cnn.com/interactive/specials/0006/genome.glossary/glossary.html

Talking Glossary of Genetic Terms—National Human Genome Research Institute
http://anthro.palomar.edu/mendel/mendel_1.htm

Websites

Access Excellence—The U.S. National Health Museum
http://www.accessexcellence.org/

Ancestry.com
http://www.ancestry.com/learn/library/article.aspx?article=4662

Blazing a Genetic Trail
http://www.hhmi.org/genetictrail/

Gene Almanac
http://www.dnalc.org/home.html

Genetic Research: A Health Spotlight Focus—Online NewsHour
http://www.pbs.org/newshour/bb/health/july-dec99/gene_therapy_splash.htm#

Genetic Science Learning Center
http://learn.genetics.utah.edu/units/basics/tour/inheritance.swf

Genographic project—National Geographic and IBM
https://www3.nationalgeographic.com/genographic/

History of Genetic Research—New York Online Access to Health
http://www.noah-health.org/en/genetic/genetics/concerns/history.html

Human Genome Project—US Department of Energy
http://www.ornl.gov/sci/techresources/Human_Genome/home.shtml

Mendel's Genetics
http://anthro.palomar.edu/mendel/mendel_1.htm

Report on Genome Research—The World Health Organization
http://www.who.int/mediacentre/news/releases/release34/en/index.html

Science—Genetics Resources for Kids
http://www.kidsturncentral.com/links/geneticslinks.htm

Books

Glass, Susan. *Genetics—Reading Essentials in Science*. Logan, Ia: Perfection Learning, 2005.

O'Brien, Robert. *Mrs. Frisby and the Rats of NIMH*. New York: Aladdin, 1986.

Shelley, Mary. *Frankenstein* (Norton Critical Edition). New York: W.W. Norton, 1995.

Torr, James, ed. *Genetic Engineering: Opposing Viewpoints*. Farmington Hills, Mich: Greenhaven Press, 2000.

Movies and documentaries

The Secret of NIMH, 1982

Jurassic Park, 1993

Gattaca, 1997

Cracking the Code of Life, 2001 (available for download or online viewing)
http://www.pbs.org/wgbh/nova/genome/program.html

Genes on the Menu, 2002 (available for download or online viewing)
http://www.firstscience.tv/sc/view/genes-on-the-menu-71.html

The Future of Food, 2004

Debate resources

Meany, John and Kate Shuster. *Speak Out! Debate and Public Speaking in the Middle Grades*. New York: IDEA Press, 2005.

Middle School Public Debate Program
www.middleschooldebate.com
Comprehensive debate instruction for the classroom and competitive contests.

Glossary

argument　　　statement designed to prove a point. It includes an assertion, reasoning, and evidence (A–R–E)

biodiversity　　variety of life forms within a habitat or ecosystem

biotechnology　method of technological scientific investigation that uses the living materials

cell　　　　　basic unit of all living organisms. Each cell of a human being contains the entire human genome. There are more than 100 trillion cells in a human being.

chromosome　　one of the threadlike structures formed of DNA and protein that carries the genes that determine heredity

cloning　　　　reproduction of an identical genetic copy

cross-breeding　method used to produce a hybrid, or mixed living organism, from two other organisms

DNA　　　　　abbreviation for deoxyribonucleic acid. Shaped like a double helix (twisted ladder), this molecule contains the hereditary material, the genetic characteristics, that are passed from one generation to the next. Each person, with the exception of identical twins, has their own unique DNA code.

epidemiology　branch of medicine that looks at where and in what numbers cases of different diseases occur

ethics　　　　rules that are used to respectfully treat other persons and living creatures. In genetic research, these include the use of voluntary and informed research subjects, a duty to protect any human involved in an experiment, privacy protection of medical information or biological materials, and professional responsibility by lab workers, doctors, and scientists.

gene　　　　　section of DNA that carries specific hereditary information, such as eye color or risk of disease. The Human Genome Project discovered that there are about 23,000-25,000 in the human body.

genome	all the genetic information and instructions used to create and maintain a living organism
heredity	genetic transfer of biological material from a parent to an offspring
Mendel's Laws	principles of heredity established in the 19th century by Gregor Mendel
methodology	using a particular method or set of rules when doing something, for example, scientific methodology
moderator	someone who presides over an event and makes sure the rules are followed
mutation	error in the replication, or copying, of DNA that produces a change in the development of an organism. Mutations can improve a living organism, damage it, or even kill it.
refutation	challenging an argument using reasoning and evidence
trait	characteristic or feature that is passed on from parent to offspring (for example, eye color or height)
variation	genetic change. A new organism can result from variation or change of the genes of the original.
weapons of mass destruction (WMDs)	These are weapons that could kill or injure hundreds or even many thousands of people. They include biological weapons (e.g., anthrax or smallpox), chemical weapons (e.g., mustard and sarin gas), radiological weapons (explosives that include radioactive elements, such as "dirty bombs"), and nuclear weapons (weapons that use uranium fission to produce many tens of thousands of tons of explosive force). Because of the spread of genetic research and genetic labs throughout the world, there is increasing concern about the use of biological WMDs, which might include the creation of powerful new versions of viruses, such as smallpox or ebola.
xenotransplantation	medical procedure in which an organ from one species is transferred into the body of another species. Most past efforts have failed immediately, but the transfer of chimpanzee and baboon hearts to humans with failing hearts has prolonged life for a few weeks.

Index